Important: Do not remove this
date due reminder.

DATE DUE

THE LIBRARY STORE   #47-0205

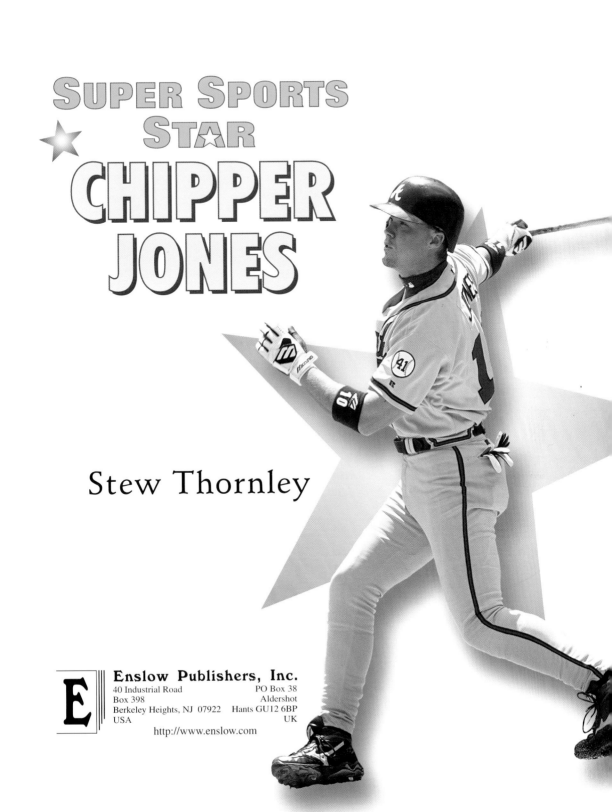

SUPER SPORTS STAR

CHIPPER JONES

Stew Thornley

Enslow Publishers, Inc.

40 Industrial Road
Box 398
Berkeley Heights, NJ 07922
USA

PO Box 38
Aldershot
Hants GU12 6BP
UK

http://www.enslow.com

Library of Congress Cataloging-in-Publication Data

Thornley, Stew.
  Super sports star Chipper Jones / Stew Thornley.
    p. cm. — (Super sports star)
  Summary: A biography of the professional baseball player whose rookie year with the Atlanta Braves in 1995 culminated in a World Series victory.
  Includes bibliographical references and index.
  ISBN 0-7660-2134-3
  1. Jones, Chipper, 1972–   —Juvenile literature. 2. Baseball players—United States—Biography—Juvenile literature.
  [1. Jones, Chipper, 1972–   . 2. Baseball players.]   I. Title.
  II.Series.
  GV865.J633T56   2004
  796.357'092—dc21
  [B]

                                          2002155208

Printed in the United States of America

10 9 8 7 6 5 4 3 2 1

To Our Readers: We have done our best to make sure all Internet Addresses in this book were active and appropriate when we went to press. However, the author and the publisher have no control over and assume no liability for the material available on those Internet sites or on other Web sites they may link to. Any comments or suggestions can be sent by e-mail to comments@enslow.com or to the address on the back cover.

Photo Credits: © 2002 Louis DeLuca/MLB Photos, p. 25; © 2002 Grieshop/MLB Photos, pp. 15, 31; © 2001 Allen Kee/MLB Photos, p. 28; © 2002 Allen Kee/MLB Photos, p. 38; © 2002 MLB Photos, pp. 4, 13, 20, 46; © 2000 Rich Pilling/MLB Photos, p. 18; © 2001 Rich Pilling/MLB Photos, p. 1; © 2002 Rich Pilling/MLB Photos, pp. 6, 10, 23, 41; © Fred Vuich/MLB Photos, p. 33; © 2001 Fred Vuich/MLB Photos, p. 9; © John Williamson/MLB Photos, pp. 36, 44.

Cover Photo: © 2001 Rich Pilling/MLB Photos.

CONTENTS

Introduction 5

1 Heating Up. 7

2 Growing Up with the Game 11

3 Mastering the Minors 21

4 Leading the Braves to the Top 26

5 Becoming the Best 32

6 Reaching for the Top 39

Career Statistics 43

Where to Write 44

Words to Know 45

Reading About and
Internet Addresses 47

Index 48

Introduction

Chipper Jones is a hard-hitting baseball player. He plays for the Atlanta Braves. Jones is a switch-hitter. That means he can bat both right-handed and left-handed.

In addition to hitting the ball, Jones draws a lot of walks. That happens a lot with good hitters. Sometimes pitchers are afraid to give them a good pitch to hit. They end up walking them instead. Getting on base by a walk also helps a player's team.

In the field, Jones can play many different positions. This makes him valuable. He used to play shortstop. When he got to the major leagues, the Braves needed a third baseman. Jones switched to that position. In 2002, Jones moved to left field. It is great for a team to have a player who is so flexible.

At the plate, Jones hits the ball hard. He often hits home runs. But he says, "I'm never going to see myself as a home-run hitter. That's the fastest way to mess up your stroke—trying to be what you're not."

Heating Up

Chipper Jones's team was hot. The Atlanta Braves had the best win-loss record in the major leagues. The Braves were in first place in the National League East Division. No other team in the division was close to them.

Jones was not as hot, at least when it came to hitting home runs. For the last four years, he had hit more than 30 home runs each season. It did not look like he would reach that total in 2002. Near the end of July, the Braves ended a road trip and came back to Atlanta. Jones had only 10 home runs.

He was doing well in other areas. His on-base percentage was over .400. He was getting a lot of hits and a lot of walks.

Even though Jones did not think of himself as a home-run hitter, others did.

They wondered why he was not hitting more long balls.

But, as the temperature got hotter in Atlanta, so did Jones. He started hitting more home runs and getting on base with hits and walks.

On August 3, the Braves played the St. Louis Cardinals. The game was scoreless in the first inning. Atlanta had a runner on base. Cardinals pitcher Matt Morris threw Jones a fastball. Jones sent it back even faster. The ball came down over the fence in right-center field. Atlanta led, 2–0.

In the fifth inning, Jones came up with a runner on base. Morris threw him another fastball. Jones hit this one over the center-field fence for another two-run homer. Atlanta went on to win the game, 6–1.

Jones had 5 home runs in his last seven games. "Now he looks like the old Chipper, the All-Star Chipper Jones," said Atlanta manager Bobby Cox.

Jones was happy with his power surge, too. "It's a little too late to say I'm going to approach my power numbers of the past, but I'd sure like to ride this way as long as I can."

With Jones on fire, it was going to be a great ride for the entire team.

The crowd loves when Chipper Jones hits home runs.

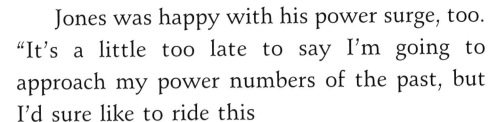

CHAPTER 2

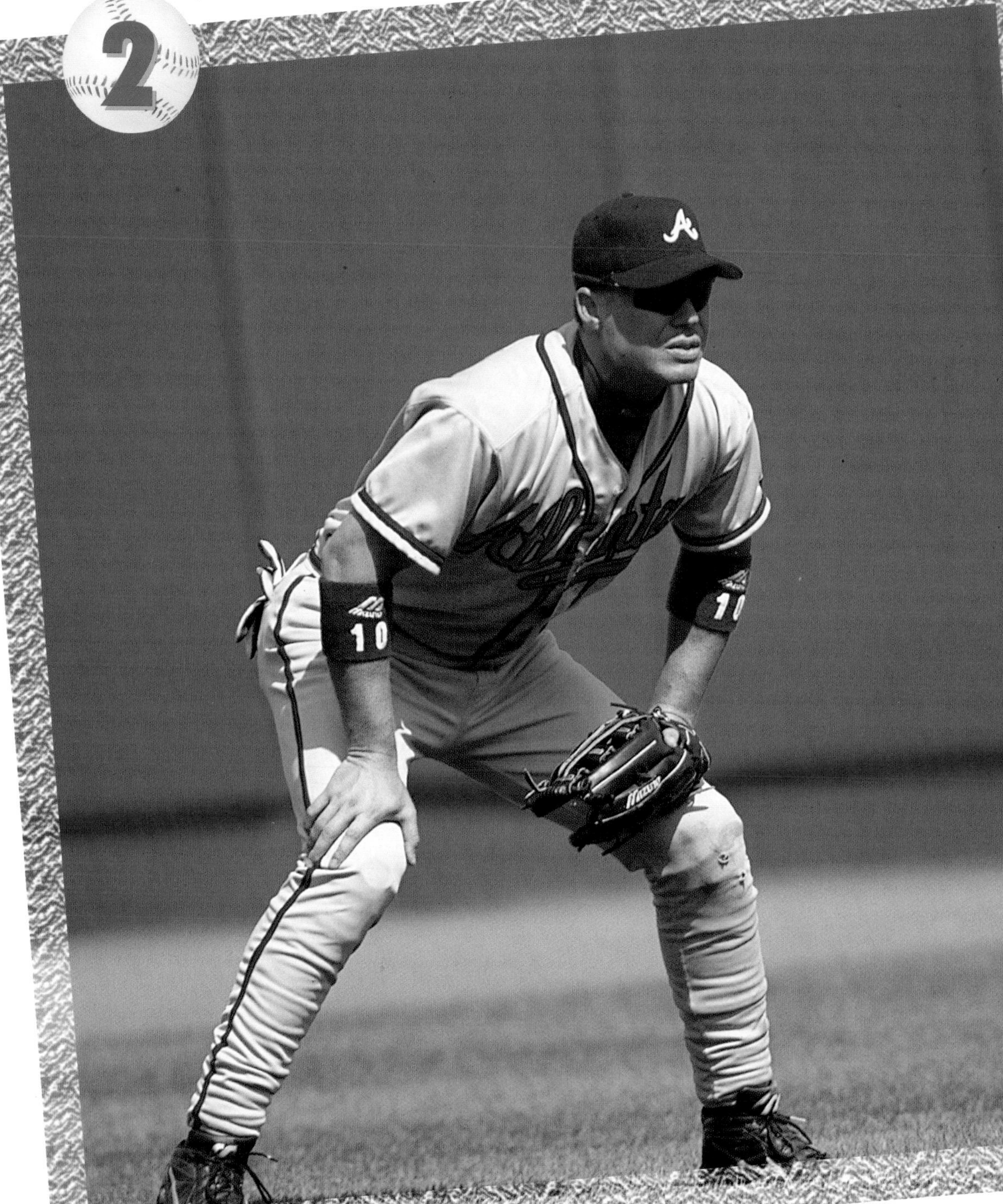

Growing Up with the Game

Larry Wayne Jones, Jr. was born April 24, 1972. His dad's name is also Larry Wayne Jones. The two are a lot alike. The younger Jones was called a "chip off the old block." From that came his nickname—Chipper.

Chipper's dad, Larry, had been a pretty good baseball player. He was a shortstop who was once drafted by the Chicago Cubs. Larry went to college instead. He then became a math teacher and high school baseball coach.

Chipper Jones loved baseball as much as his dad. "Dad has always been my idol. When I found out he was a shortstop, that's what I wanted to play," Jones said.

The Joneses lived in Pierson, Florida. Larry was the baseball coach at Taylor High School.

Chipper often went to those practices, even though he was still in grade school. When they got home, Chipper and Larry went into the yard and played baseball with one another. Larry hoped his son would someday have the chance to play professional baseball. He worked hard to help Chipper learn the game.

Larry Jones taught his son to be a switch-hitter. A switch-hitter can bat from either side of the plate. It can be an advantage for a left-handed hitter to bat against a right-handed pitcher. Likewise, it can be an advantage for a right-handed hitter to bat against a left-handed pitcher. In their yard, Larry pitched to Chipper and had him bat left-handed and right-handed from the time that Chipper was six or seven years old.

In real games, though, Chipper usually hit only right-handed. When he played Little League baseball, Jones says he probably did not come to bat left-handed more than ten times. As he got used to it, Jones started hitting more

Chipper helped his high school baseball team win their state championship.

from both sides. By the time he made the high school team, he was switch-hitting all the time.

Lynne Jones often joined her husband and son in the backyard games. "She usually didn't pitch to me," Jones said of his mother, "but she'd play at first base so I could practice my throws across the infield."

When Chipper was ready to play on the Taylor High School team, his dad had a problem. Larry was coach of the baseball team. He knew his son was good enough to play on the team even though he was only in eighth grade. But if Larry let his son play, it might look like he was playing favorites. Larry stepped down as coach. Chipper made the team on his own.

Later, Larry thought his son was having it too easy at Taylor High, both in the baseball field and in the classroom. He transferred Chipper to The Bolles School. It is a private school in Jacksonville, Florida, about ninety miles from Pierson.

Being a switch-hitter
can have its
advantages.

Away from home, Chipper was not happy. But Larry told him to stick with it. Once he got used to it, Chipper did well in school. He did even better playing baseball. He led Bolles to the state championship baseball game for three years in a row. Each year, Bolles eliminated Taylor High from the playoffs. "There was a lot of pressure to do well in those games," he said. "I couldn't go away to another school, come back, and lose."

Jones did well in other sports, too. He was a powerful golfer and a great receiver on the Bolles football team. But his baseball skills were the ones that really stood out.

Not only was he a great shortstop, Jones was also a terrific pitcher. As a junior, Jones had a win-loss record of 11–1. Bolles won the state title that year. The team came close to another championship the next year. However, Bolles lost in the championship game. Jones had a batting average of .477 when he was a senior. He hit 5 home runs, drove in 27 runs, and scored 45 runs. Don Suriano, the baseball coach at Bolles, said, "If a coach gets one like him in a lifetime, he's lucky. I'd be surprised if he doesn't make it in the big leagues."

Jones was looking ahead. High school and college teams use aluminum bats. Players in professional baseball use wooden bats. Jones started using a wooden bat in practice so he would be ready for pro ball.

Many scouts from major-league teams attended Bolles games when Jones was a senior. Even Bobby Cox, the general manager of the Atlanta Braves, came to see Jones. The Braves had the first pick in the draft. Jones hoped the Braves would take him. There were no major league teams in Florida at this time. Atlanta was the closest team to Florida. "I'd be ecstatic if Atlanta drafted me," Jones said, "because it would be easier for my dad to see me play."

Jones got his wish. Atlanta made him the top pick in the 1990 draft. Jones was happy. So were the Braves. "We're delighted to get a

Chipper was drafted as the number one pick by the Atlanta Braves in the 1990 draft.

shortstop of his ability," said Cox. "He already has excellent defensive ability, along with tremendous speed and the ability to switch-hit. We feel he's a high-quality talent at a position that's difficult to fill."

Jones thought of his family when he was drafted. "I believe 100 percent that my dad wants me to be a big leaguer," he said. "He always said the happiest day of his life will be when he walks into a major league stadium and hears my name over the loudspeaker."

Larry Jones was already thrilled at what his son had done. "We've been very fortunate with Chipper," he said. "When people say, 'Chipper reminds me of you,' I couldn't be prouder."

Mastering the Minors

The year before the Braves drafted Jones, they finished in last place. In 1990 they finished last again. They could use a good new player. But Jones was still too new. The Braves wanted to make sure he did well in pro ball, and they did not want to rush his progress. Like most players, Jones began in the minor leagues.

Jones started with the Bradenton team in the Gulf Coast League. It was the lowest level of the minor leagues. Even so, Jones struggled. He hit only one home run and had a batting average of .229. Even worse, he made a lot of errors at shortstop.

The next year, Jones was with the Macon Braves in the South Atlanta League. He hit much better. His batting average was .326. He had 15 home runs and 98 runs batted in (RBIs). He also led the league by scoring 104 runs. Jones was named the league's Player of the Month in June. He was the starting shortstop for the All-Star team. However, Jones still had trouble in the field. He made 56 errors.

Jones started the 1992 season with the Durham Bulls in the Carolina League. It is a Class A League. Class A is one of the lowest levels of minor-league baseball. Halfway through the season, Jones was moved up to Greenville, which plays in Class AA. He was a step closer to the major leagues.

The higher level did not slow Jones down. He got a hit in each of his first eight games. Jones ended up with a batting average of .346 with 9 home runs in the 67 games he played for Greenville.

In 1993, he was with the Richmond Braves. Richmond is in the International League, a Class AAA league—one step below the major leagues. Jones was great. He led the league in runs scored, hits, and triples. He did so well that the Atlanta Braves called him up to the majors near the end of the season. He played in eight games but came to bat only four times. However, he had a walk and 2 hits in those trips to the plate.

Jones still had trouble at shortstop. He had led the International League in errors. The Braves kept him in the majors in 1994. But they planned to play him in left field. It was not just that Jones had made a lot of errors at shortstop. The Braves already had a steady player, Jeff Blauser, at that position.

Chipper Jones was going to start in left field for the Braves instead of at shortstop.

There were more problems for Jones, though. In a spring training game, Jones tore a ligament in his left knee. It was a serious injury. He needed surgery. It also meant he would miss the entire 1994 season.

"It was my first summer ever without playing baseball," he said. Jones worked very hard to recover from the injury. He spent time in the weight room. Not only did the knee get better, Jones added weight and muscle. He was bigger and stronger than ever. And he was ready to help the Braves in 1995.

Leading the Braves to the Top

At the start of the 1990s, the Atlanta Braves were a last-place team. They turned that around quickly. Atlanta made it to the World Series in both 1991 and 1992. They lost the World Series both years. They continued winning, but they still had not gotten the big prize. The team hoped 1995 would be its year.

The Braves were happy to have Jones healthy and ready to help them. They also had a new position for him. It was third base. "His attitude was, whatever is best for the team," said Bobby Cox, who was now the Atlanta manager.

Jones hit his first major-league home run on May 9. It was in the top of the ninth inning at New York, and it won the game for the Braves.

It also started a home run spree for Jones. He had four more over the next week. On May 20, he hit a game-winning home run in the bottom of the ninth. He was off to a great start. He also played well at third base.

Jones finished the regular season with 23 home runs. He led the Braves in runs scored and tied for the team lead in walks. Atlanta finished first in the National League West Division. The Braves had the best record in the National League. However, they had to win two playoff rounds to get to the World Series.

The Braves played the Colorado Rockies in the first playoff series. The first game was in Colorado. Jones homered in the game, and the Braves had a 4–3 lead in the eighth inning. However, the Rockies scored in the last of the eighth to tie the game. They looked like they would score more. With runners on first and third and no out, Andres Galarraga hit a grounder down the third-base line. Jones dove to his right. He flopped on his stomach, reached

Chipper helps his team at bat by hitting home runs.

out, and snagged the ball in his glove. He then threw to second for a force-out. He also kept the runner on third from scoring. He twisted his knee. But he stayed in the game. "My knee would have to be hanging by a thread for me to come out of the game," he said.

The game stayed tied into the ninth. Jones changed that. He hit another home run. The Braves won the game, 5–4.

In the second game, Colorado had a 4–3 lead after eight innings. Jones led off the top of the ninth with a double. It was his third hit of the game, and the start of a four-run rally for the Braves. Atlanta won, 7–4.

Colorado won the third game and had a 3–0 lead in the next one. Jones doubled home two runs. Fred McGriff then hit a two-run homer. The Braves went on to win the game and the playoff series. Jones hit 4 home runs and had a .389 batting average in the series.

Atlanta next played the Cincinnati Reds for the league pennant. The Reds led, 1–0, after eight innings. Jones started the ninth with a single and came around to score the tying run. The Braves won the game in 11 innings. Atlanta went on to win the series with the Reds. Jones hit .438 in those games. The playoff victory put the Braves in the World Series.

The Atlanta Braves went on to win the World Series against the Cleveland Indians. This was the first win for the Braves since 1957, when the team played in Milwaukee.

For Chipper Jones, it was a great way to finish off his first full year in the majors. Jones's teammates on the Braves knew how much he helped them win. One of the players, Walt Weiss, said of Jones, "Every time I see him, he impresses me more."

Becoming
the Best

Jones had a great rookie season in 1995. He did even better the next few years. He hit 30 home runs and drove in 110 in 1996. He also scored 114 runs. Jones played in the All-Star Game and got a hit. The Braves made it back to the World Series. This time, though, they lost to the New York Yankees.

The Braves had a new stadium in 1997. In the first game at Turner Field on April 4, Jones got the first hit. He had another outstanding season leading the Braves with 100 runs scored and 111 runs batted in. He stole bases and was not caught stealing all season. The Braves finished with 101 wins during the regular season. They had the best record in baseball. However, they were beaten in the second round of the playoffs and did not make it to the World Series.

The same thing happened in 1998. This time the Braves won 106 games, the most in the National League. Jones got off to a fast start. From April 13 to April 19, he hit 5 home runs

Chipper Jones is ready
to make the catch.

and drove in 13. He was named National League Player of the Week. Jones was voted by the fans to start in the All-Star Game. He finished the season with a batting average of .313 with 34 home runs. Jones was getting on base a lot and helping his team to be one of the best in the game.

However, for the second year in a row, the Braves were defeated in the league playoffs.

Jones and the Braves wanted to get back to the World Series in 1999. Jones got off to a slow start, but he heated up in May. Atlanta was doing well, but so were the New York Mets. The teams were in a battle for the top spot in the National League East Division.

Jones got even hotter as the season went into its final month. He drew at least one walk in sixteen straight games from August 19 to September 5. That tied a National League record. In September, the Braves and Mets met for a three-game series. It was an important set of games.

In the first game of the series, Jones hit a home run. It was the Braves' only run, and the game was tied, 1–1, in the eighth inning. Then Jones hit another home run. The Braves won the game.

In the first inning of the next game, Jones got his team off to a quick start with a two-run homer in the bottom of the first. The Braves went on to win, 5–2. If they could win the next day, they would be almost certain to win the division title. In the fifth inning of that game, the Mets were ahead by a run. Jones changed that. He hit a three-run homer. The Braves won the game and swept the series.

Jones finished the season with a batting average of .319. He hit 45 home runs, scored 116, drove in 110, and walked 126 times. He set a National League record for the most home runs and most walks by a switch-hitter in a season. His biggest performance came in those big games against the Mets in September. After

Chipper Jones set a National League record for most home runs by a switch-hitter in a season.

the season, Jones was voted as the National League's Most Valuable Player.

The Braves did better in the league playoffs and made it back to the World Series. They played the New York Yankees, the team that had beaten them in the 1996 World Series. The Yankees did it again, beating the Braves to win the world championship.

Atlanta knew it would have more chances to win the World Series again. Their best player was still only twenty-seven years old. Chipper Jones had many great years in front of him.

Reaching for the Top

In 2000, Jones was elected to be the starting third baseman in the All-Star Game. The game was played at Turner Field. Jones would be in front of his home fans. He came through, hitting the only home run of the game for either team. He had hits in his other two trips to the plate, too.

He also did well during the regular season. He scored at least 100 runs and drove in more than 100 for the fifth straight year. Atlanta finished first again in the National League East. They had finished first every year Jones had been with them. But they did not do as well in the postseason. They were knocked out in the first round by the St. Louis Cardinals.

It was more of the same in 2001. The Braves had another huge year by Jones and another first place finish during the regular season only to get knocked out during the league playoffs.

The Braves got a new player to help them in 2002. It was Vinny Castilla, a good hitter. Castilla played third base, so the Braves switched Jones to left field. Just as he had done when he first came up, Jones moved to another position to help the team.

The Braves won 101 games in 2002. They had the best record in the National League. Jones hit 26 home runs and drove in 100 runs. He had a batting average of .327 and also drew more than 100 walks. But Atlanta was again defeated in the first round of the playoffs.

By the end of July 2003, the Braves had the best record in baseball. Jones was having another good year. He hoped he could get the Braves back to the World Series again.

When he is not playing baseball, Jones enjoys hunting and fishing. He is involved in the community. Jones set up the Chipper Jones Family Foundation to help young people. Jones's foundation works with organizations like the Cystic Fibrosis Foundation and Boys & Girls Clubs of America.

Jones also has a family of his own. He and

Chipper tries his best and will continue to help lead the Braves.

his wife, Sharon, have a son, Larry Wayne Jones III. Jones also has another son named Matthew.

Jones works very hard to be the best player he can be. He studies the game and learns everything he can about the pitchers he will be batting against. His teammates come to him for advice, too. When Jones talks baseball, other members of the Braves listen.

Although he works hard at it, Jones has a lot of fun playing baseball. Even when a lot is riding on the outcome of a game, Jones stays relaxed and has a good time.

He knows how good he is, but he does not brag. His confidence helps him when he plays in an important game. "I've been through a lot of pressure games in my life," he says. "Some guys live for crunch time. I'm one of them."

CAREER STATISTICS

												MLB
Year	Team	G	AB	R	H	2B	3B	HR	RBI	BB	SB	Avg.
1993	Atlanta	8	3	2	2	1	0	0	0	1	0	.667
1995	Atlanta	140	524	87	139	22	3	23	86	73	8	.265
1996	Atlanta	157	598	114	185	32	5	30	110	87	14	.309
1997	Atlanta	157	597	100	176	41	3	21	111	76	20	.295
1998	Atlanta	160	601	123	188	29	5	34	107	96	16	.313
1999	Atlanta	157	567	116	181	41	1	45	110	126	25	.319
2000	Atlanta	156	579	118	180	38	1	36	111	95	14	.311
2001	Atlanta	159	572	113	189	33	5	38	102	98	9	.330
2002	Atlanta	158	548	90	179	35	1	26	100	107	8	.327
TOTALS		1,252	4,589	863	1,419	272	24	253	837	759	114	.309

G—Games
AB—At Bats
R—Runs
H—Hits

2B—Doubles
3B—Triples
HR—Home Runs
RBI—Runs Batted In

BB—Bases on Balls (Walks)
SB—Stolen Bases
Avg.—Batting Average

Where to Write to Chipper Jones

Mr. Chipper Jones
c/o Atlanta Braves
P.O. Box 4064
Atlanta, Georgia 30302

Chipper Jones continues to be a great baseball player for the Braves.

WORDS TO KNOW

at bat—A player gets an at bat when he comes to the plate and gets a hit, makes an out, or reaches base on an error. He does not get an at bat if he walks, is hit by a pitch, sacrifices, or hits a sacrifice fly.

draft—A selection of players by major-league teams, which take turns choosing the players they want.

extra-base hit—A hit that is longer than a single. A double, triple, or home run is an extra-base hit.

free agent—A player who is free to sign with any team.

intentional walk—A walk where the pitcher intentionally throws pitches outside the strike zone.

leadoff—The first player in the batting order.

rookie—A player in his first full season in professional sports.

sacrifice—A player gets a sacrifice when he bunts for the purpose of advancing another base runner. If he does this, he is not charged with an at bat, and it does not hurt his batting average.

sacrifice fly—A player gets a sacrifice fly when he hits a fly that allows a base runner to tag up and score after the catch. As with a sacrifice, the player is not charged with an at bat, and it does not hurt his batting average.

senior—A twelfth-grade student in high school or a fourth-year student in college.

wild-card team—The second-place team in each league with the best record. Since the mid–1990s, the wild-card team makes the playoffs.

Chipper Jones is a great outfielder.

READING ABOUT

Books

Buckley, Jr., James. *Play Ball!* New York: DK Publishing, 2002.

Murray, Jim. *Chipper Jones*. Broomall, Penn.: Chelsea House Publishers, 1999.

Potts, Steve. *Atlanta Braves*. North Mankato, Minn.: Smart Apple Media, 2001.

Weber, Bruce. *Baseball Megastars 1998*. New York: Scholastic, 1998.

Zack, Bill. *Chipper Jones*. Philadelphia, Penn.: Chelsea House Publishers, 1999.

Internet Addresses

The Official Web Site of the Atlanta Braves
  <http://atlanta.braves.mlb.com/NASApp/mlb/index.jsp?c_id=atl>

The Official Website of Chipper Jones
  <http://www.chipperjones.com>

INDEX

A

Atlanta Braves, 5, 7–8, 17, 21, 23, 24, 26–42

B

Blauser, Jeff, 23
Bolles School, 14, 16–17
Bradenton Braves, 21

C

Castilla, Vinny, 39
Cincinnati Reds, 29–30
Cleveland Indians, 30
Colorado Rockies, 27, 29
Cox, Bobby, 8, 17, 19, 26

D

Durham Bulls, 22

G

Galarraga, Andres, 27
Greenville Braves, 22

J

Jones, Larry III (son), 40
Jones, Larry, Sr. (father), 11–12, 14, 16, 19
Jones, Lynne (mother), 14
Jones, Sharon (wife), 40

M

Macon Braves, 21

McGriff, Fred, 29
Morris, Matt, 8

N

New York Mets, 34, 35
New York Yankees, 32, 37

R

Richmond Braves, 22

S

St. Louis Cardinals, 39
Suriano, Don, 17
switch-hitter, 5, 12, 14, 19, 35

T

Taylor High School, 11, 14, 16

W

Weiss, Walt, 30